READING AND WRITING

Sourcebook

Authors

Ruth Nathan

Laura Robb

Great Source Education Group

a division of Houghton Mifflin Company

Authors

Ruth Nathan is one of the authors of *Writers Express* and *Write Away* and the author of many professional books and articles on literacy. She earned a Ph.D. in reading from Oakland University in Rochester, Michigan, where she co-headed their reading research laboratory for several years. She currently teaches the third grade and consults with numerous schools and organizations on reading. Ms. Nathan recently spoke in front of the U.S. Senate on the topic of best practices.

Laura Robb is the author of *Reading Strategies That Work; Summer Success: Reading; Literacy Links; Teaching Reading in Social Studies, Science, and Math;* and *Teaching Reading in the Middle School* and has taught language arts at Powhatan School in Boyce, Virginia, for more than 30 years. She also mentors and coaches teachers in Virginia public schools and speaks at conferences throughout the country.

Table of Contents

I Am an Apple

By Jean Marzollo

What do you know about apples?

You cane eat APPle.

Where have you seen apples?

At the Farm.

What color is each apple? Write the colors below.

 red

  green

 Yellow

Predict and Preview

Now look at the title of the reading on page 8. What does it tell you about the reading?

How APPles can grow.

Look at the pictures in the reading. Then look through the whole reading. What do the pictures tell you about the reading?

rain HelP seeds grow.

MY PURPOSE

What will I learn about apples?

STUDYING WORDS: COLOR WORDS

What are the words for each of these colors?

Draw a line from each color to the word for it.

Red

Blue

Yellow

Green

Orange

Purple

Pink

Brown

II. READ

Now read *I Am an Apple* by Jean Marzollo.
1. Read it once all the way to the end.
2. Then, read it again. This time, whenever the apple changes, write the change in "My Notes."
3. Then complete the "Stop and Explain" boxes.

My Notes

Example:

red

I Am an Apple
by Jean Marzollo

I am a red bud.

I live on a branch in an apple tree.

I grow in the rain.

I grow in the sun.

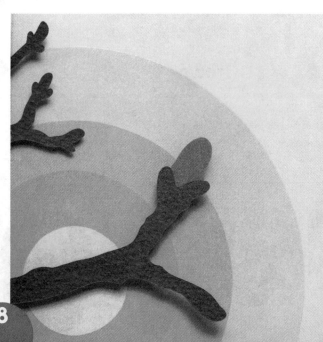

I Am an Apple (continued)

I unfold.

I'm an apple blossom!

I have five petals.

I am beautiful.

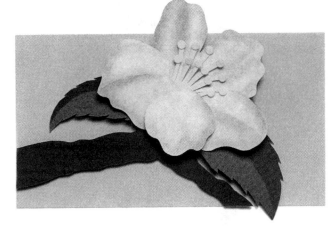

In time, my petals fall to the ground.

Now I am a small apple.

I hang by a stem.

The stem brings me water and food.

I grow bigger and bigger.

STOP and EXPLAIN

What are two things that have happened to the apple? Use your notes.

I Am an Apple (continued)

My tree is full of apples.

Once we were green.

Now we are red.

Red, redder, reddest.

We are ready to be picked!

STOP and EXPLAIN

What did you learn about apples?

WORD WORK — Short a

The words *apple* and *cat* have a **short a** sound. Say each word sound by sound: a pp le, c a t. Listen to the vowel sound. That's the **short a** vowel sound.

Now read the words below. Say each word. If it has the **short a** sound, write it in the **"short a"** column below. Write it under Other Sounds if it has another vowel sound.

> man   his   with   rat   pop   rug
> crack   bat   flap   put

Short a Sound

Other Sounds

WORD WORK Adding *er* or *est*

The word *strongest* has a suffix. The suffix *est* is added to *strong* to make a new word. Look at these examples.

cold + er = colder   strong + est = strongest

Now look at these words.

red + er = redder
big + est = biggest

Did you notice that both of these words doubled the final consonant before adding the suffix?

Now add suffixes to these words.

green + est = _____

sad + d + er = _____

soft + est = _____

pink + er = _____

III. DRAW AND WRITE

Think about what you learned about apples. Draw two ways that the apple changed.

1.

2.

Now write a sentence about apples.

Mice Squeak, We Speak

By Arnold L. Shapiro

Think of an animal. What kind of sound does it make?
Draw the animal. Above your picture, write a word for
the sound.

I. BEFORE YOU READ

Preview

Before you begin, look at the reading on page 18. Use the checklist to learn all that you can before you begin reading.

PREVIEW CHECKLIST

- ☐ **Title**
- ☐ **First Sentence**
- ☐ **Pictures or Photos**
- ☐ **Last Sentence**

What did you learn from your preview?

_____

_____

_____

_____

_____

_____

MY PURPOSE

What are some noises that animals make?

STUDYING WORDS: PLURALS WITH *S* OR *ES*

In English, we usually add *s* or *es* to the end of a word to show that it is plural.

hat

hats

fish   **fishes**

Add *s* to these words to make them plural.

truck
trucks

car
cArs

Add *es* to these words to make them plural.

box
boxes

dish
Dish

Now read *Mice Squeak, We Speak* by Arnold L. Shapiro.
1. Read it all the way through once.
2. Then, come back and read it again. In "My Notes" on each page, write a question you have.
3. Next, complete the "Stop and Draw" boxes.

My Notes

Example:

What does a hoot sound like?

Mice Squeak, We Speak
by Arnold L. Shapiro

Cats purr.

Lions roar.

Owls hoot.

Bears snore.

Crickets creak.

18

Mice squeak.

STOP and DRAW

Draw one of the animals in the story.

Sheep baa.

But I SPEAK!

Monkeys chatter.

Cows moo.

Ducks quack.

Doves coo.

Pigs squeal.

Horses neigh.

Chickens cluck.

But I SAY!

Flies hum.

Dogs growl.

Bats screech.

Coyotes howl.

Frogs croak.

Parrots squawk.

Bees buzz.

But I TALK!

STOP and DRAW

Draw something you saw in the story.

The word *hum* has a **short u** sound. Say *hum*—h u m —to yourself. Do you hear the sound in the middle?

Now look at these pictures and read each word below. Each word has the **short u** sound. Circle the letter in each word that makes the **short u** sound.

cup

truck

duck

Read these words. Write them in two groups in the columns below. Put the words with **short u** in one group. Write the other words in the other group.

cluck	rock	buzz	spot	chat	but

Short u Sound | Other Sounds

WORD WORK Plurals with *s* or *es*

Words that are plural usually end in *s* or *es*. Circle the words below that are plurals.

1. (lions)
2. (bears)
3. boat
4. house

5. (fishes)
6. cow
7. (horses)
8. place

Now add *s* to these words to make them plural.

chicken **duck** **boat** **frog**

1. chickens
2. Duck

3. boats
4. frog

Now add *es* to these words to make them plural.

wish **fox** **kiss** **box**

1. wishes
2. foxes

3. Kisses
4. Boxes

III. DRAW AND WRITE

Draw a picture of a place outside with some animals.

Now write a sentence that tells about what you drew. Use plurals if you drew more than one animal.

Bread, Bread, Bread

By Ann Morris

What is bread? Answer these questions about bread.

Yes   **No**   **A roll is a kind of bread.**

Yes   **No**   **Bread that is cooked is called toast.**

Yes   **No**   **All bread is white.**

Yes   **No**   **Bread comes in one shape—a loaf.**

Draw a picture of what bread looks like to you.

I. BEFORE YOU READ

K-W-L

Before you begin, look at the reading.

Write one thing you know about bread under **K** (*know*).

Write a question about what you want to learn about bread under **W** (*want to learn*).

Then, come back after you read and write one thing you learned about bread under **L** (*learn*).

KNOW

WANT

LEARN

MY PURPOSE

What are some different kinds of bread?

STUDYING WORDS: WORDS WITH *ING*

The spelling of some words doesn't change when you add *ing*. For instance, *call* becomes *calling*. Look at these words after adding *ing*.

1. know ⟶ know**ing**
2. help ⟶ help**ing**
3. start ⟶ start**ing**
4. pull ⟶ pull**ing**

Now try writing some *ing* words of your own. Add *ing* to each of these words and write them on the lines.

truck	pick	say	crunch	soak

1.

2.

3.

4.

5.

II. READ

Now read *Bread, Bread, Bread* by Ann Morris.
1. Read it once just for fun.
2. Then read it again. In "My Notes," write something you know about bread. See the example.
3. Then complete the "Stop and Draw" boxes.

My Notes

Example:

My family eats bread all the time.

Bread, Bread, Bread
by Ann Morris

People eat bread all over the world.

There are many kinds, many shapes, many sizes—

skinny bread,

fat bread,

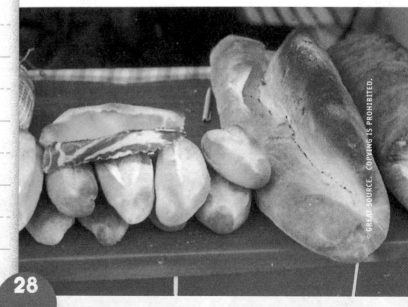

BREAD, BREAD, BREAD (continued)

round flat bread,

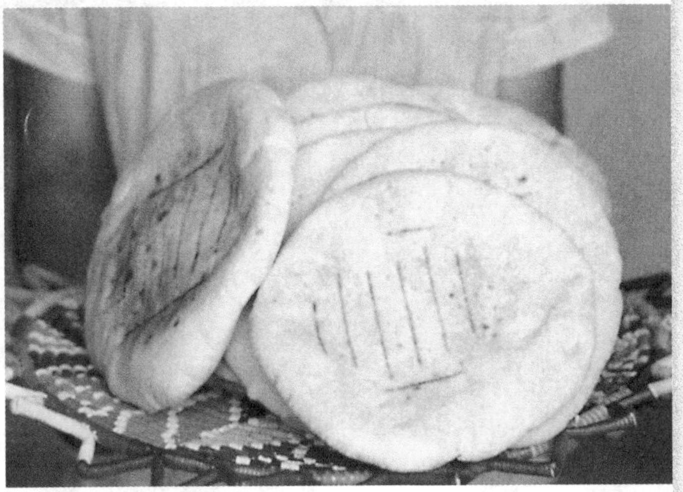

bread with a hole,

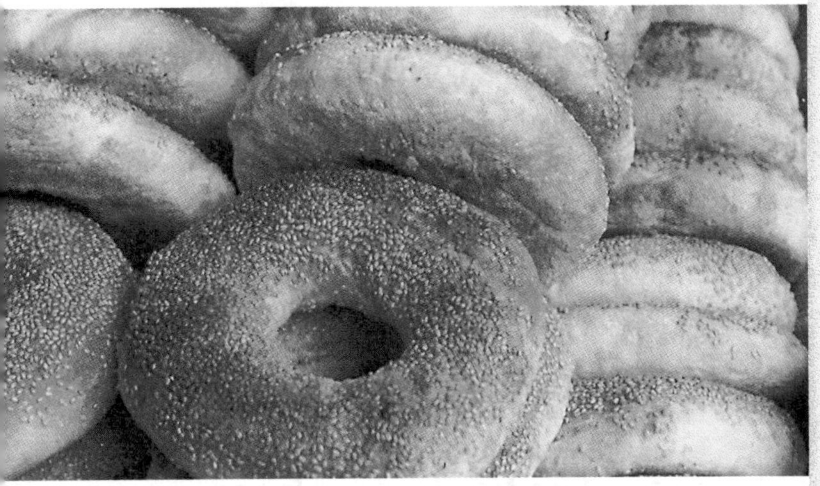

crunchy bread,

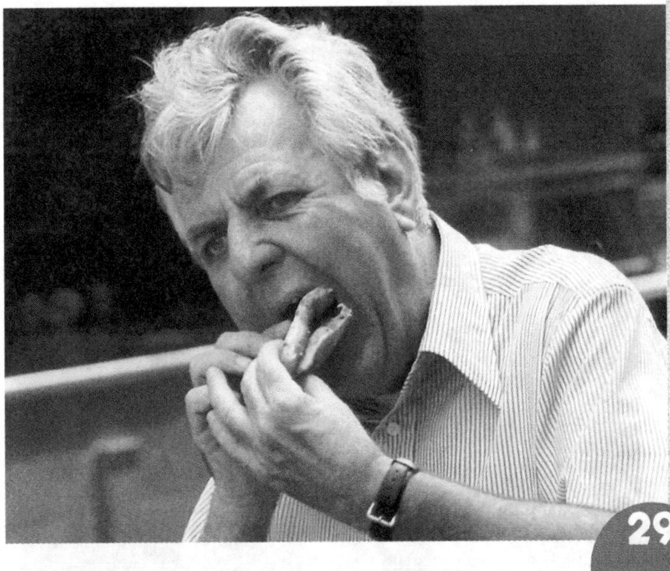

My Notes

lunchy bread . . .

and bread to soak up your egg.

Pizza, pretzel . . . they are bread too.

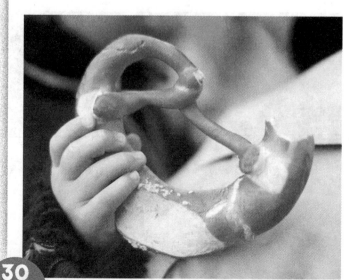

Bread on the table . . .

Bread on your head.

Bread is good for you.

It helps you grow.

It makes you strong.

My Notes

STOP and DRAW

Draw two kinds of bread you really like. Write names for your drawings.

The word *fat* has the **short a** sound. Say *fat* one sound at a time: f a t. Can you hear the sound in the middle? That's the **short a** sound.

Circle the word in each list that has the **short a** sound.

1. cap

bed

bug

2. head

rock

bat

3. lip

man

sock

Now read the words with the **short a** sound below. Circle the letter that spells the **short a** sound.

sang   pat   map   sat

32

WORD WORK   Adding y Endings

Did you see the word *crunchy* in the reading? It is the word *crunch* with *y* added. Some words add the ending *y* when they describe things. Describing words are called adjectives.

Look back at the reading. Look for adjectives that end in *y*, like *crunchy*. Write at least 2 of them here.

_____

_____

_____

_____

Now make these words adjectives by adding the *y* ending to them.

junk	stuff	might

_____

_____

_____

_____

III. WRITE

Go back to *Bread, Bread, Bread* and find your favorite words. On the web below, write some words from the story and some of your own words that describe bread.

WORD FROM THE STORY

YOUR OWN WORD

WORD FROM THE STORY

YOUR OWN WORD

Now write a sentence, using words from your web. Tell something you learned about bread.

Sam's Story

By Edward Marshall

Which animals get along with each other? Which ones don't?

Read each sentence and circle whether it is true or false. Share your ideas with a partner.

True **False** Dogs like to chase cats.

True **False** Cats like to chase mice.

True **False** Cats will chase birds.

True **False** Birds and dogs always get along together.

True **False** All animals are friends.

Word Web

What do you know about cats? Use the web below to write three things you know about cats.

cats

MY PURPOSE

What is Sam's story and who is it about?

STUDYING WORDS: CONTRACTIONS

Sometimes two words are shortened into one word. The new word is called a contraction. Here are some examples. Notice that an apostrophe replaces the missing letters.

do not ——→ don't

I am ——→ I'm

you will ——→ you'll

they are ——→ they're

Now read these words. Cross out the ones that are not contractions.

| that's | he'll | do not | isn't | would not | she |

Write the contraction for each pair of words below. Look at the second word in each pair. First, cross out the letters you won't use. Put the rest of the letters together. Add an apostrophe where you took out letters.

he is

she will

we have

Now read "Sam's Story" by Edward Marshall.
1. First, read the story all the way to the end.
2. Then read it again. This time think about what you see in your mind. Draw a picture of it in "My Notes" and complete the "Stop and Retell" boxes.

My Notes

"Sam's Story"
by Edward Marshall

A rat went for a walk.

"What a fine day," he said.

"The sun is shining and all is well."

My Notes

Soon he came to a shop.

"My, my," said the rat. "What a pretty cat. And I have never had a cat."

"I will buy that cat and have a friend," he said.

And he went into the shop.

"I want a cat," he said.

"Are you sure you want a *cat*?" asked the owner.

"I am sure," said the rat. "And I want that one."

"That will be ten cents," said the man. "If you are *sure*."

"I am sure," said the rat. "Here is my last dime. Give me my cat."

The rat and the cat left the shop.

"SAM'S STORY" (continued)

"We will be friends," said the rat.

"Do you think so?" said the cat.

"Well, we'll see."

The rat and the cat sat in the sun.

"What do you do for fun?" asked the rat.

"I like to catch things," said the cat.

STOP and RETELL

Write one thing that has happened so far.

"That's nice," said the rat.

"I am hungry," said the cat. "How about lunch?"

"A fine idea," said the rat. "What is your favorite dish?"

"I do not want to say," said the cat.

"You can tell me," said the rat. "We are friends."

"SAM'S STORY" (continued)

"Are you *sure* you want to know?" said the cat.

"I am sure," said the rat. "Tell me what you like to eat."

"I will tell you," said the cat. "But let us go where we can be alone."

"Fine with me," said the rat.

STOP and RETELL

What do you think will happen next?

The cat and the rat went to the beach.

"I know," said the rat. "Fish."
"You like to eat fish."

"Not at all," said the cat. "It's much better than fish."

"Tell me," said the rat. "I just *have* to know."

"Come closer," said the cat. "And I will tell you."

"Yes?" said the rat.

"SAM'S STORY" (continued)

"What I like," said the cat, "is . . .

. . . CHEESE! I love cheese!"

"So do I," said the rat. "And I have some here."

"Hooray!" said the cat. "And now we are friends."

So they sat on the beach and ate the cheese.

And that was that.

STOP and RETELL

What surprised you at the end?

The word *shop* in "Sam's Story" has the **short o** sound.
Say *shop*: sh o p. Can you hear the middle sound?

These words all have the **short o** sound. Circle the vowel
in the middle that makes the **short o** sound.

top	stop	lock
mop	box	hop

Find three words with the **short o** sound in the list
below. Then write those three words below.

pop	junk	job
jump	sing	sock

1.

2.

3.

Now use one of the words in a sentence.

WORD WORK — Suffixes *ed, er, ing*

Did you see the words *asked* and *owner* in the story? Each word has a word ending called a suffix.

ask ⟶ **asked**   own ⟶ **owner**

A word changes meaning when a suffix is added. Some common suffixes are *ed*, *er*, and *ing*.

ed	er	ing
talked	darker	speaking
started	brighter	asking
warmed	colder	showing

Add the suffix to each word below to make a new word. Then write the new word.

help + ed =

want + ing =

add + ed =

calm + er =

III. WRITE

Think about the cat and the rat in "Sam's Story." Write two words that tell about each character.

cat

rat

Now write two sentences. Write one sentence that tells something about the cat. Then write a sentence that tells something about the rat.

5

Shoes, Shoes, Shoes

By Ann Morris

What kind of shoes do you have? Write some of the different kinds on the web below.

shoes

I. BEFORE YOU READ

Preview

Before you read, look ahead to page 52. See what the reading will be about. Check off each item in the Checklist as you preview *Shoes, Shoes, Shoes*.

CHECKLIST

- ☐ Title
- ☐ First few words or first sentence
- ☐ Pictures or photos
- ☐ Last few words or last sentence

MY PURPOSE

What are shoes for? How many kinds of shoes are there?

STUDYING WORDS: PLURALS

The reading is about shoes. The word *shoes* ends in *s* because it means "more than one." That's what a plural is—more than one.

Here are some other words that are plural.

years	**things**	**numbers**
words	**songs**	**days**

Now look at some more words for things that you wear. Add *s* to each word to make it plural and write it.

shirt + s =

belt + s =

sock + s =

hat + s =

sweater + s =

II. READ

Now read *Shoes, Shoes, Shoes* by Ann Morris.
1. Read it all the way through once.
2. Then read it again. In "My Notes," write a question you have as you read.
3. Then do the "Stop and Draw."

My Notes

Example:

Where can you find shoes?

Shoes, Shoes, Shoes
by Ann Morris

Shoes, shoes, all kinds of shoes, wherever you find them, shoes come in twos!

Old shoes,

My Notes

new shoes,

just-right-for-you shoes.

Work shoes,

play shoes,

any-time-of-day shoes.

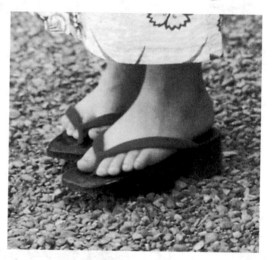

There are school shoes

and dancing shoes,

My Notes

walking shoes and
riding shoes,

shoes for the ice, and
shoes for the snow.

Shoes keep your feet
dry wherever you go.

STOP and DRAW

Stop and think about what you have read. Draw what you
remember.

Read the words with short vowel sounds below. What sound do you hear in the middle of each one?

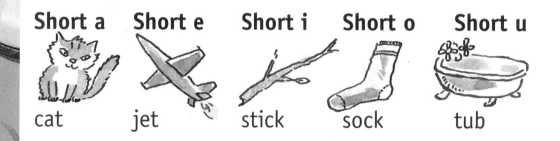

Short a	Short e	Short i	Short o	Short u
cat	jet	stick	sock	tub

All of these words have short vowel sounds, too. Write them under the right heading. Then read each list aloud and listen to the short vowel sound.

hand	box	pet	run
fit	red	black	pin

Short a

Short e

Short i

Short o

Short u

WORD WORK   Adding s

The words *kinds* and *shoes* are both plural. They have an *s* added to the end. That shows they mean "more than one."

Now make some plurals of your own. Add *s* to each of the words below to make them plural.

pen

pet

coat

hand

letter

DRAW AND WRITE

Draw three shoes that you wear or see.

Now write three sentences. Tell about the things you drew above.

6

Building a House

By Byron Barton

What is a house?

What are other words for *house*?

Write words that describe houses.

house

Predict and Preview

Look ahead to page 62. Read the title, the first sentence, and all of the pictures. Now write three things you predict you will learn about building a house.

1.

2.

3.

MY PURPOSE

Who are the people who make houses? What do they do?

STUDYING WORDS: COMPOUNDS

You can take two small words and put them together to make a new word. The new word is a **compound word**.

These words are from *Building a House*. Find each compound word in the story and circle it. Talk about the meaning of each word with a partner.

COMPOUND WORDS	TWO SMALL WORDS
bricklayer	**brick + layer**
fireplace	**fire + place**
inside	**in + side**

READ

Now read *Building a House* by Byron Barton.
1. Read the story once all the way through.
2. Then, read it again. Underline the names of who or what helps build a house. In the "My Notes" column, write those words.
3. Then complete the "Stop and Retell" box.

My Notes

Example:

bulldozer

Building a House
by Byron Barton

On a green hill

a bulldozer digs a big hole.

© GREAT SOURCE. COPYING IS PROHIBITED.

BUILDING A HOUSE (continued)

Builders hammer and saw.

A cement mixer pours cement.

Bricklayers lay large white blocks.

My Notes

STOP and RETELL

Below are names of machines that help build a house.
Write what each one does.

Machine	What It Does
bulldozer	
cement mixer	

STOP and RETELL

My Notes

Carpenters come and make a wooden floor.

They put up walls.

64

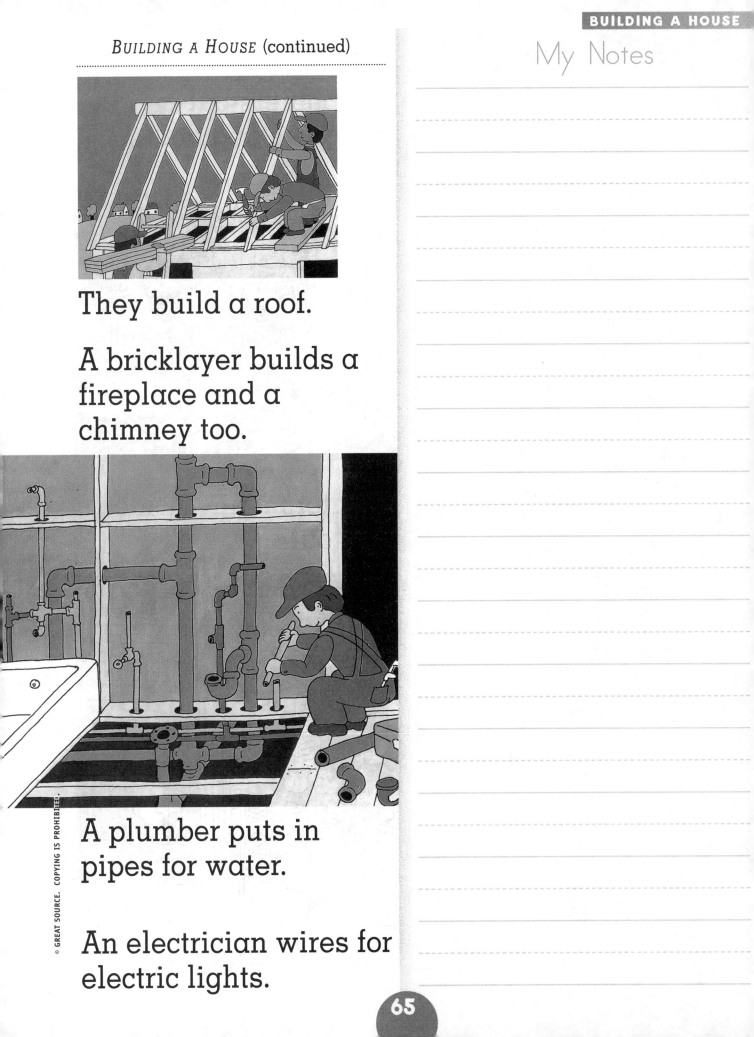

They build a roof.

A bricklayer builds a fireplace and a chimney too.

A plumber puts in pipes for water.

An electrician wires for electric lights.

My Notes

My Notes

Carpenters put in windows and doors.

Painters paint inside and out.

The workers leave.

BUILDING A HOUSE (continued)

The house is built.

The family moves inside.

REREAD

Below are names of people that help build a house. Write what each one does. You might have to reread parts to find out.

Person	What He or She Does
carpenter	
bricklayer	
painter	

Read the words in the box. Each word has the **short i** sound. Write each word in the column that names the same word family.

Clue: Words in the same family have some of the same letters.

Word Box:

sink	drill	big	lip	rink	dig	fill

ill	ip	ig	ink

Now find three words from page 62 of *Building a House* that have a **short i** sound. Then write them.

1.

2.

3.

WORD WORK Compounds

The words below are compound words. Each one is made up of two smaller words. Draw a line between the two words in each compound.

COMPOUND WORD BOX

houseboat	cupboard
nightlight	doghouse
tabletop	flashlight
skyscraper	wallpaper
doorbell	within

Now find and write three compound words from *Building a House*.

1. _____

2. _____

3. _____

III. DRAW AND WRITE

Draw a picture of one thing you learned about building a house.

Write 3 sentences about your picture.

7

Water

By Frank Asch

Where can you find water? On the web below, write four places you can find water.

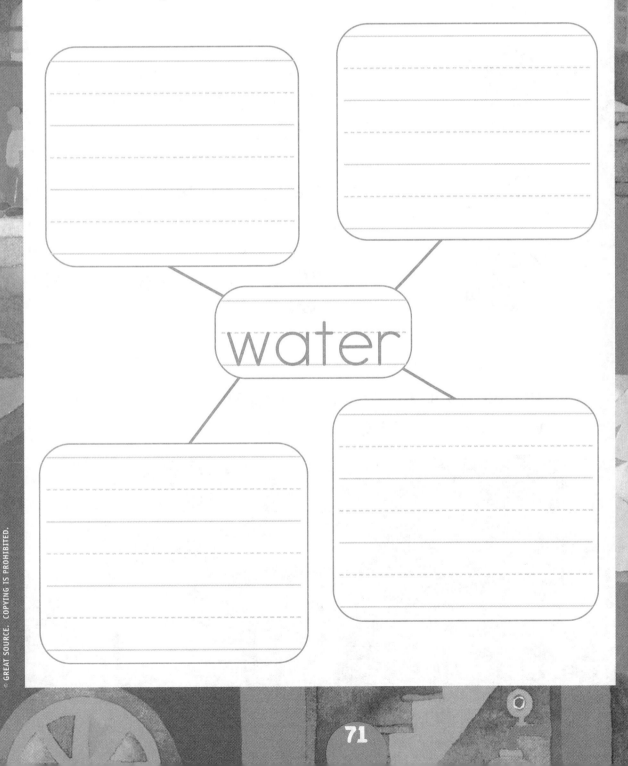

What Do You Know?

What do you already know about water? Try this short quiz to find out how much you already know.

 Yes   No   **There is water in snow.**

 Yes   No   **The water in a river is different from the water in a lake.**

 Yes   No   **Water is in clouds.**

Yes   No   **When you cry, a tear is just water.**

Now discuss your answers with a partner. Tell each other why you answered the questions the way you did.

MY PURPOSE

What is in water and where do we find it?

STUDYING WORDS: WORDS WITH *ER* OR *EST*

Read these words.

tall   **taller**   **tallest**

Do you see the endings *er* and *est*? They are added to some describing words called adjectives to show comparison.

Write the word that best fits each picture below.

shorter   **short**   **shortest**

bigger   **big**   **biggest**

Now read *Water* by Frank Asch.

1. Read through *Water* one time.
2. Then come back and read it a second time. As you do, draw 3 things you want to remember in "My Notes."
3. Then complete the "Stop and Draw" boxes.

My Notes

Water
by Frank Asch

Water is rain.

Water is dew.

Water is ice and snow.

Water is high in the sky.

WATER (continued)

Water is deep in the earth.

Water is a tiny brook growing bigger and bigger.

Water is a waterfall and mist.

STOP and DRAW

Look back at what you have read so far. Then draw something you have read about.

Water is a small pond and a large lake.

Water is what fish *breathe* . . .

. . . and flowers *drink*.

Water is a salty tear.

Water is a flood.

WATER (continued)

Water is a long, winding river . . .

. . . flowing to the sea.

My Notes

STOP and DRAW

Now go back and read *Water* once more. When you finish, draw something below that helps you remember what you read.

What vowel sound do you hear in the words *sky* (s k y), *high* (h i g h), *tie* (t i e), and *ice* (i c e)? The sound you hear is **long i.**

Complete the sentences below. Use only the words from the box that have a **long i** sound.

cry	old	cake	pie
nice	low	high	spy

In this _____

apple _____ ,

a _____ has left me a message.

It says, "Climb _____ and

don't _____."

WORD WORK | Dividing Words in Syllables

How many beats do you hear in the word *water*? You probably heard two beats—wa / ter. These beats are syllables. Each syllable has one vowel sound. Listening for syllables in words you hear will help you read and spell words.

One-syllable Words

rain   sea   tear   ice

Two-syllable Words

water   salty   growing   tiny

Three-syllable Words

waterfall   Saturday   fisherman

Now read the words below. Listen for the beats in each one. Then write whether it has one, two, or three syllables.

cry _____   rainy _____

Sunday _____   remember _____

unhappy _____   lake _____

III. WRITE

Ask two classmates this question:

Where can you find water?

Look back at your web on page 71. Now finish this paragraph by telling where you can find water.

You can find
water in many places.

Too Many Rabbits

By Peggy Parish

Look at the rabbits shown here. What can you tell about rabbits from the picture? Write three things you can tell about them.

Three things about rabbits

1.

2.

3.

Predict

Look at the title of the reading on page 84. Then look at the beginning of the story and the pictures.

Now predict what this story will be about. Circle True or False for each statement.

True   **False**   This story will be about a small girl.

True   **False**   This story could really happen.

True   **False**   This story is about a family of rabbits.

MY PURPOSE

Why is the story title
Too Many Rabbits?

STUDYING WORDS: ADDING *S* OR *ES* TO WORDS

Look at the words *door* and *doors*.

- How are their meanings different?
- How are their spellings different?

Some words are made plural by adding *s* or *es*. Write the plural of these words below.

rabbit	box	kitchen	wish

rabbit _____

box ___ _____

kitchen _ _____

wish __ _ _____

II. READ

Now read the story *Too Many Rabbits* by Peggy Parish.
1. Read the story all the way through.
2. Then come back and read it again. This time write in "My Notes" how this is like something in your life.
3. Then complete the "Stop and Think" boxes.

My Notes

Example:

I had a friend come over, too.

Too Many Rabbits
by Peggy Parish

Thump! Thump! Thump!

"Now what is that?" said Miss Molly.

Thump! Thump! Thump!

"There it is again," said Miss Molly.

"I had better see what it is."

Miss Molly went to her door.

She opened it.

There sat a fat rabbit.

"Goodness me!" said Miss Molly.

"Where did you come from?"

TOO MANY RABBITS (continued)

The rabbit looked at Miss Molly.

Then she looked at the open door.

"Oh well," said Miss Molly.

"Come in if you like."

But the rabbit was already in.

STOP and THINK

Write what happens first.

"I will feed you," said Miss Molly. "Then you must go home."

So Miss Molly fed the rabbit.

"All right," she said.

"Out you go."

She opened the door.

But the rabbit hopped the other way.

"So you came to stay," said Miss Molly.

"Well, you may stay tonight. But tomorrow you must go. I will fix a box for you."

And she did.

The rabbit hopped into the box.

Miss Molly went to bed.

Soon she was asleep.

My Notes

Next morning Miss Molly got up.

She went to the kitchen.

The rabbit was still in the box.

"Did you have a good night?" said Miss Molly.

The rabbit said nothing.

"Here is your breakfast," said Miss Molly.

The rabbit did not move.

"You are a lazy one," said Miss Molly.

She went over to the rabbit's box.

And what a surprise she had.

She saw not one rabbit.

She saw a box full of them.

"Oh dear!" said Miss Molly.

STOP and THINK

Write what you think will happen next.

TOO MANY RABBITS (continued)

"Baby rabbits! Lots of baby rabbits. No wonder you wanted to stay."

Miss Molly shook her head.

"Babies need lots of care. Even baby rabbits. I will have to let them stay," she said.

So all of the rabbits stayed.

My Notes

STOP and THINK

Write what happens at the end of the story.

What sound do you hear in the words *bee* (b ee), *sea* (s ea), and *she* (sh e)? That sound is called the **long e** sound.

Read these silly sentences. Mark an X in front of the ones that have words with the **long e** sound.

Silly E's

_____ **We see Bea by the sea.**

_____ **I like Mike and Spike.**

_____ **He and she eat a pea.**

_____ **Pete has sweet feet.**

Write the words below that answer the questions.

bee	see	pea

What do you do with your eyes?

_____

_____

What likes flowers and stings?

_____

_____

WORD WORK — Adding es to Words with y

Some words are made plural by changing a final y to i and adding es.

bunny   **bunnies**

Use the plural form of the words below to complete the crossword puzzle.

Singular	Plural
pony	ponies
sky	skies
baby	babies

Look back at *Too Many Rabbits*. Make a list of what happens in the beginning, middle, and end of the story.

beginning

middle

end

Now write a paragraph that tells what happens in *Too Many Rabbits*. Tell one thing that happens in the beginning, in the middle, and in the end.

9

Ronald Morgan Goes to Bat

By Patricia Reilly Giff

What does the picture below show? Talk about it with a partner. Then write three things that you see in the picture.

1.

2.

3.

BEFORE YOU READ

Preview

Before you read, take time to look ahead. Look at the story on page 96. Check off each of these items as you read them:

PREVIEW CHECKLIST

- ☐ **Title**
- ☐ **First sentence**
- ☐ **Pictures**
- ☐ **Last sentence**

After previewing these parts of the story, write what you think this story will be about.

_____

_____
_____

_____
_____

MY PURPOSE

Who is Ronald Morgan and what does he do?

STUDYING WORDS: WORDS WITH *ED* ADDED

Read the words below. What 2 letters do you see at the end of each word? Circle those letters.

yelled	**started**
looked	**pulled**

The ending *ed* is used to show that something happened in the past.

Present	Past
look	**looked**

Add *ed* to the following words. Use them in the sentences.

ask laugh

I _____ my mother to play ball with me.

We all _____ at the joke yesterday.

II. READ

Now read the story *Ronald Morgan Goes to Bat* by Patricia Reilly Giff.

1. Read the story all the way to the end.
2. Then come back and read the story again. This time, in "My Notes," write a question you have.
3. Then complete the "Stop and Retell" boxes.

My Notes

Example:

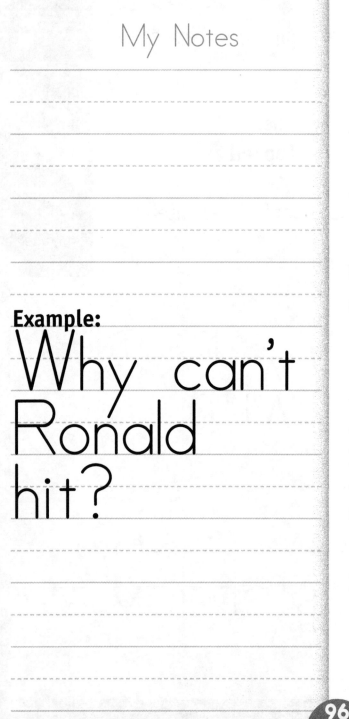

Why can't Ronald hit?

Ronald Morgan Goes to Bat

by Patricia Reilly Giff

Baseball started today.

Mr. Spano said everyone could play.

"Even me?" I asked.

And Tom said, "You're letting Ronald Morgan play? He can't hit, he can't catch. He can't do anything."

Mr. Spano looked at me.

"Everyone," he said.

"Yahoo!" I yelled.

I pulled on my red and white shirt, the one that says GO TEAM GO, and ran outside to the field.

"Two things," Mr. Spano told us.

"Try hard, and keep your eye on the ball."

Then it was time to practice.

Michael was up first.

He smacked the ball with the bat.

STOP and RETELL

Write what happened in the story so far.

The ball flew across the field."

"Good," said Mr. Spano.

"Great, Slugger!" I yelled. "We'll win every game."

It was my turn next.

I put on my helmet, and stood at home plate.

"Ronald Morgan," said Rosemary. "You're holding the wrong end of the bat."

Quickly I turned it around.

I clutched it close to the end.

Whoosh went the first ball.

Whoosh went the second one.

Wham went the third.

It hit me in the knee.

"Are you all right?" asked Michael.

But I heard Tom say, "I knew it. Ronald Morgan's the worst."

At snack time, we told Miss Tyler about the team.

"I don't hit very well," I said.

And Rosemary said, "The ball hits him instead."

Everybody laughed, even me.

I shook my head.

"I hope it doesn't happen again."

Miss Tyler gave me some raisins.

"You have to hit the ball before it hits you," she said.

Can you hear the **long o** sound in the words *go* (g o), *know* (kn ow), *mole* (m o l e), *float* (f l oa t), and *toe* (t oe)? Notice that the **long o** sound is spelled many ways.

Here are some other words that have the **long o** sound.

slow	hole	so	boat
blow	pole	no	coat

All of the words below have the **long o** sound. Use them to complete the secret message below.

rope	go	snow	no

Take this _____ and

tie it to the tree. Then _____ out into

the cold, white _____ and

spell the word _____ . I will get the

message.

WORD WORK Compound Words

Did you see the words *outside*, *everybody*, and *baseball* in the story? These are all compound words. They are made up of two smaller words.

outside ⟶ out + side
everybody ⟶ every + body
baseball ⟶ base + ball

Now look carefully at these compound words. Write the two smaller words that make up each one.

_____

everyone _____

_____

anything _____

_____

daytime _____

III. WRITE

Look back at *Ronald Morgan Goes to Bat*. What are four words you would use to tell someone about Ronald? Write them on the web.

Ronald Morgan

Now write a journal entry about Ronald. Tell three things that you have learned about Ronald Morgan. Use the words in your web.

10

The Golly Sisters Go West

By Betsy Byars

What do you think life was like in the Old West? What can you learn from the picture below?

Now write some words that tell about the Old West.

Old West

Predict and Preview

What can you learn about this story just by reading the title?

The Golly Sisters Go West

Discuss with a partner what you think this story will be about.

Now look at the pictures from the story on page 106. What's happening? What can you learn from them? Talk about these pictures with a partner.

Now predict what you think this story will be about. Write your answer here.

_____

_____

_____

_____

_____

_____

_____

MY PURPOSE

What will the Golly sisters do in the West?

STUDYING WORDS: SILENT LETTERS

You know letters stand for sounds. You can hear each letter sound in words like *pig*, *bat*, and *trip*. But in some words one or more letters are silent.

Have you ever seen silent letters in words? Look at words such as *ghost* and *wrong*. In *ghost*, the *h* is silent. In the word *wrong*, the *w* is silent.

Try to find some silent letters on your own. Circle the letter or letters in each word below that are silent.

rose

wrench

eight

knot

Talk with a partner. Then write a word you know that has a silent letter.

I. READ

Now read the story *The Golly Sisters Go West* by Betsy Byars.

1. First, read the story all the way through to the end.
2. Then read the story again. This time think about what you see as you read. Draw a picture of it in "My Notes."
3. Then complete the "Stop and Retell" boxes.

My Notes

Example:

The Golly Sisters Go West

by Betsy Byars

The Golly sisters sat in their wagon.

They were going west.

"Go," May-May said to the horse.

The horse did not go.

"This makes me mad," May-May said.

"Our wagon is ready. Our songs and dances are ready.

And the horse will not go."

"It makes me mad too," said Rose.

"Something is wrong with this horse."

STOP and RETELL

What happens first in the story?

Rose got down from the wagon.

May-May got down too.

They walked around the horse.

"Do you see anything wrong?" May-May asked.

"No, but something is wrong," said Rose.

"When we say, 'Go,' the horse does not go."

"And if the horse does not go, we do not go," said May-May.

STOP and RETELL

What has happened so far?

STOP and RETELL

Suddenly, Rose said, "Sister! I just remembered something. There is a horse word for 'go.'"

"A horse word?" said May-May. "What is it?"

"Giddy-up!" said Rose.

My Notes

The horse went.
"Stop! Stop!" cried
May-May.
"Is there a horse
word for stop?"

STOP and RETELL

What do you think will happen next in the story?

My Notes

"Whoa," said Rose.

"WHOA!" cried May-May.

The horse stopped.

The sisters got into the wagon.

Rose took the reins.

"Giddy-up, horse," she said.

The horse went.

May-May said, "Now that we know the right words, we can go west."

"Yes," said Rose. "We are on our way!"

STOP and RETELL

What happens at the end of the story?

Say the words *make* (m a ke) and *may* (m ay) from the story. What vowel sound do you hear? That's the **long a** sound.

Now say these word pairs.

can	cane
tap	tape
pan	pain

Which words have the **long a** sound? The words on the right have the **long a** sound. The **long a** sound is spelled many ways.

Now place the words below into two groups.

bake	bat	day	dad

Words with Short a

_____

_____

_____

_____

Words with Long a

_____

_____

_____

_____

WORD WORK · Adding *ed* and *ing*

In the story, some of the words have endings called suffixes. For example, *walked* has the ending, or suffix, *ed*. *Going* has the ending *ing*. The root words don't change.

Add an ending to each word below. Write the new word on the lines.

eat + ing

_____

pull + ed

_____

show + ed

_____

grow + ing

_____

tell + ing

_____

II. WRITE

What would you say if you were going on a trip? **Who** would you tell? **When** and **where** would you be going? **What** would you do there? Jot notes under each heading.

Who
_____

When
_____

Where
_____

What
_____

Now write a note. Start with **who** you are writing to and **when** and **where** you are going. Then tell **what** you will do.

Date: _____

Dear _____,

_____

_____

_____

_____

_____

_____

11

Stars

By Jennifer Dussling

Talk with a partner about the picture below. What do you know about stars?

Write two or three things you know about stars.

I. BEFORE YOU READ

Let's see how much you know about stars.

Read the sentences. Circle whether you agree or disagree with each one.

Yes	No	Stars can be red, yellow, or orange.
Yes	No	Stars can be found up in the clouds.
Yes	No	Stars give off light.
Yes	No	Stars are just very big rocks.

After you read *Stars*, come back and check your answers.

MY PURPOSE

What are stars? What are some words to describe them?

STUDYING WORDS: ANTONYMS

An antonym is an opposite. The words *hot* and *cold* are antonyms. *Cold* is not like *hot*. They are completely different.

Read these other pairs of antonyms.

soft	⟷	hard
fast	⟷	slow
light	⟷	heavy
top	⟷	bottom

Circle each pair of antonyms in the list below. Check your answers with a partner.

1. play   work
2. horse   animal
3. dark   light
4. low   high
5. large   small
6. early   late
7. run   go

Now write a pair of antonyms you know. Share your words with a partner.

_____

_____

_____

Now read *Stars* by Jennifer Dussling.
1. Read all the way through to the end.
2. Then reread *Stars*. As you do, write a question you have in "My Notes."
3. Then complete the "Stop and Explain" box.

My Notes

Example:

Why do stars look white?

Stars
by Jennifer Dussling

Look at the night sky. What do you see? Lots and lots of white dots.

Stars!

Long ago some people said the sky was like a bowl turned upside down.

It sat on the tops of mountains.

The stars were holes—holes poked in the bowl.

STARS (continued)

Some people made up stories about the stars.

One group of stars looked like a crown.

People said it was the crown of a princess.

A god loved the princess.

But then she died.

The god put her crown in the sky—so he could see it forever.

Today we know what a star really is.

A star is a ball of burning gas.

It is very hot and very bright.

What would you tell a friend about stars?

_____

_____

_____

_____

_____

_____

My Notes

STARS (continued)

Stars come in different colors. There are yellow stars and blue stars. There are red stars and orange stars too.

But when you look up at the sky, most stars look white.

Stars are big—very, very big.
They only look small because they are so far away.

STARS (continued)

Think of the biggest star and Earth like this.

You have a soccer ball in one hand.

That is the big star!

You have one little grain of sand in your other hand.

That is Earth.

One star is closer than the rest.

It is not the biggest star.

But it looks big because it is so near.

We feel its heat.

This star is the sun.

STOP and RETELL

What two things can you explain about stars?

Words like *sky* (s k y), *white* (wh i t e), *night* (n igh t), and *side* (s i de) all have the **long i** sound. Can you hear it?

What letter or letters help to make the **long i** sound in these words?

Circle the words in the lists below that have the **long i** sound.

cry	bite	why	did
right	kite	if	sight
it	write	fry	fright

Now find the two words below that have the **long i** sound. Then write them.

try	if	like	with

_____   _____

WORD WORK Homophones

Say the words *hole* and *whole*. Now say the words *see* and *sea*. What do you notice about each pair of words?

_____

_____

_____

_____

_____

Words that sound alike but have different spellings are called **homophones**. The meaning of the word in a sentence tells you how to spell it.

Circle the right word in each sentence.

Today I will (by, buy) my lunch.

You do not (no, know) the answer.

Please bring (to, two) pencils to class.

Take about (for, four) steps and stop.

My dad (red, read) me a story yesterday.

Write a pair of homophones you know.

_____

_____

WRITE

Now plan to write a paragraph describing stars.

First, write the most important thing you would tell someone about stars. This will be your main idea.

Then write two words that describe stars.

Main Idea

1.

2.

Write your paragraph describing stars below.

Duckling Days

By Karen Wallace

Look at the picture of the mother duck and her ducklings. How would you describe the ducklings? Write three or four words below to describe the ducklings.

I. BEFORE YOU READ

Predict and Preview

From the title *Duckling Days*, what do you think it will be about?

From the art on page 128, what do you think the reading will be about?

What do you think will happen in this reading?

MY PURPOSE

What are duckling days and what are they like?

STUDYING WORDS: VOWEL SOUNDS WITH *R*

What letter do all of these words have in common?

car	bird	short
hurt	shirt	arm

All of the words above have the letter *r*. When words have a vowel and *r* together, the *r* changes the vowel sound.

Can you hear the vowel sound? Try to group the words below into two groups: Short Vowels or Vowel Sounds with *r*.

burn	man	pig	bug
farm	girl	hen	corn

Short Vowels	Vowel Sounds with *r*

Now read the story *Duckling Days* by Karen Wallace.
1. Read the story all the way through first.
2. Then come back and read the story again. This time write in "My Notes" how the story is like your life.
3. Then complete the "Stop and Retell" boxes.

My Notes

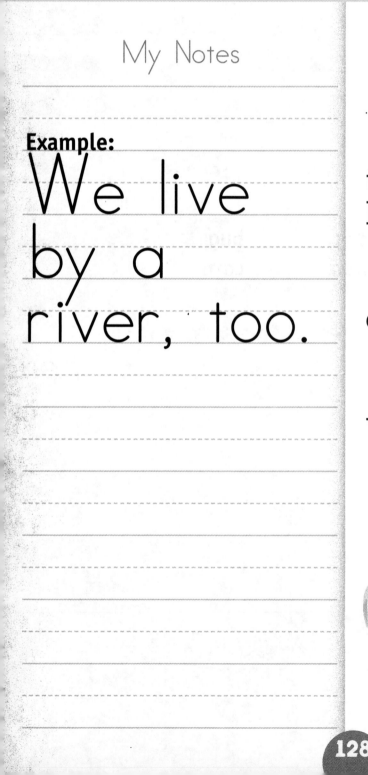

Example:
We live by a river, too.

Duckling Days
by Karen Wallace

In the grass beside the river a mother duck builds her nest.

She gathers grass and makes a hollow.

She lines her nest with downy feathers.

DUCKLING DAYS (continued)

In a nest beside the river a mother duck lays six white eggs.

She keeps them warm beneath her body.

Inside each egg a duckling grows.

My Notes

STOP and RETELL

What happens first in the story?

A duckling hatches from his egg.
He cracks the shell.

He makes a hole with his tiny beak.

He taps and pushes.

He breaks out of the shell and squeezes out.

STOP and RETELL

What happens next in the story?

DUCKLING DAYS (continued)

Other ducklings hatch beside him.

At first their legs are weak and wobbly.

Their down feathers are wet and sticky.

They dry out quickly near their mother.

STOP and RETELL

What happens at the end of the story?

WORD WORK Short Vowels

The words *duck* and *nest* in the story have short vowels.

Group the words below under the vowel sound you hear in the middle of each word. Use the four guide words to help you hear the short vowel sounds.

shell	fun	tap	six
grass	with	nest	duck

hat

pen

win

bug

WORD WORK Adding *y* or *ly*

In *Duckling Days*, find the words *downy* and *wobbly*. Note the *y* and *ly* at the end of these words.

Watch how these words added the ending.

down + y = downy   quick + ly = quickly

Now try to make some new words by adding *y* or *ly*. Write the new word you can make.

_____

soft + ly _____

fuzz + y _____

slow + ly _____

dirt + y _____

nice + ly _____

WRITE

Retell the story *Duckling Days*. Start by writing what happens in the beginning, middle, and end of the story.

Beginning
Write what happens on page 128 here.

_____

_____

_____

_____

Middle
Write what happens on pages 129–130 here.

_____

_____

_____

_____

End
Write what happens on page 131 here.

_____

_____

_____

_____

13

Clean Your Room, Harvey Moon!

By Pat Cummings

What does your room look like? Draw a picture of your room when it gets messy.

BEFORE YOU READ

Word Web

Close your eyes and think a minute about cleaning your room. What comes to mind?

On the web below, write three or four things you have to do when you clean your room.

Cleaning Your Room

MY PURPOSE

What happens when Harvey Moon cleans his room?

STUDYING WORDS: DIVIDING TWO-SYLLABLE WORDS

You can read big words.
You just need to know how to break
them into small parts called **syllables**.

mitten

This word has two syllables: mit / ten.

Try to divide these words. Divide them into syllables by
drawing a line between the two consonants in the middle
of each word.

dancer   hollow

dripping   grabbing

picture   pillow

hammer   letter

Listen to the first vowel sound in each word. Is it a short
sound or a long sound?

_____

_____

_____

_____

_____

II. READ

Now read *Clean Your Room, Harvey Moon!* by Pat Cummings.
1. Read the story all the way through one time.
2. Then read the story again. This time, in "My Notes," respond to the questions you see.
3. Then complete the "Stop and Retell" boxes.

My Notes

Question:
How is Harvey feeling?

He feels good.

Clean Your Room, Harvey Moon!
by Pat Cummings

On Saturday morning
    at ten to nine
Harvey Moon was
    eating toast,

Waiting for the
    cartoon show
That he enjoyed the
    most.

With only minutes
    left to go,
He heard the voice of
    DOOM.

"Today, young man,"
    his mother said,
"Is the day you clean
    your room!"

Question:
What would Harvey rather be doing?

"Not nowwww . . ."
  moaned Harvey,
Red in the face.

"I'll miss 'Rotten Ed'
And 'Invaders from
  Space!'"

"Right this second!"
  she ordered,
And gave
  him the
  broom.

Harvey
  marched
  angrily
Up to his room.

It really didn't seem
  Messy at all.

First he'd throw his
  dirty clothes
Out in the hall.

Under the bed was
An ice cream-
  smeared shirt,

My Notes

Jeans that had what
   Mom called
"Ground-in dirt. . . ."

Two towels and
   swim trunks
That seemed to be wet,

Three socks he
   sniffed
And found weren't
   dirty yet.

Under the dresser
   was a lump
Warm and gray,

STOP and RETELL

What two things have happened in the story so far?

1.

2.

CLEAN YOUR ROOM, HARVEY MOON! (continued)

That he didn't
  recognize
So he put it away.

The floor of the
  closet had clumps
Hard and dirty

Of T-shirts and
  sweatshirts . . .
IT WAS TEN-THIRTY!

Harvey panicked
  then thought,
"I should be through
  soon,

I'll eat lunch while I
  watch
'Creature Zero' at
  noon."

Grabbing marbles
  and crayons and
Flat bottle caps,

Two of his own
  special
Lightning bug traps,

My Notes

Question:
How does Harvey feel now?

The softball he
    couldn't find
Last Saturday,
One toothbrush, one
    helmet . . .
He put them away.

"I'll clear out these
    toys
And then I'll be done,

'Ken's Kung Fu
    Korner'
Will be on at one. . . ."

Under his desk were
    some comics
All icky

From something
    inside
That was dripping
    and sticky.

He found library
    books
He'd forgotten he
    had,

His skates from Aunt
    Sarah,
His bow tie from dad,

He found a caboose
That was missing its
    train,

A whistle,
    paintbrushes,
A map of the brain.

STOP and RETELL

What are two more things that have happened in the story?

3.

4.

WORD WORK — Long Vowel Review

What vowel sound do you hear in *throw* and *most*? Can you hear the **long o** sound?

What vowel sound do you hear in *tie* and *nine*? Can you hear the **long i** sound?

Long vowels sound like the letter.

long a	sounds like *a*
long e	sounds like *e*
long i	sounds like *i*
long o	sounds like *o*

Say each word below. Listen to the vowel sound in it. Then write the word in the correct box.

toast	bike	brain	tie
most	skates	clean	eat

long a

long e

long o

long i

WORD WORK Contractions

Words like *I'll*, *he'd*, *didn't*, and *couldn't* are called contractions. They are shortened forms of two words.

I will	=	I'll
he had	=	he'd
did not	=	didn't
could not	=	couldn't

Did you see the apostrophe (') in the contractions? It shows that one or more letters are missing. Notice which letters are missing.

Read each set of words below. Then write the contraction you can make from them.

1. he will = _____

2. she had = _____

3. would not = _____

4. should not = _____

WRITE

Use the web below to name some words to describe a messy room.

```
┌──────────────────────┐        ┌──────────────────────┐
│                      │        │                      │
│ - - - - - - - - - -  │        │ - - - - - - - - - -  │
│                      │        │                      │
└──────────────────────┘        └──────────────────────┘
              ╲          ┌──────────────┐         ╱
               ╲         │  Messy Room  │        ╱
               ╱         └──────────────┘        ╲
┌──────────────────────┐        ┌──────────────────────┐
│                      │        │                      │
│ - - - - - - - - - -  │        │ - - - - - - - - - -  │
│                      │        │                      │
└──────────────────────┘        └──────────────────────┘
```

Write a poem about a messy room, using some of the words you wrote.

Messy rooms
are

They

Wilhe'mina Miles After the Stork Night

By Dorothy Carter

Wilhe'mina Miles is a story about a little girl and her family.

What do you think she and her family will be like? Look at the pictures in the story on page 150. Write three or four words that describe Wilhe'mina.

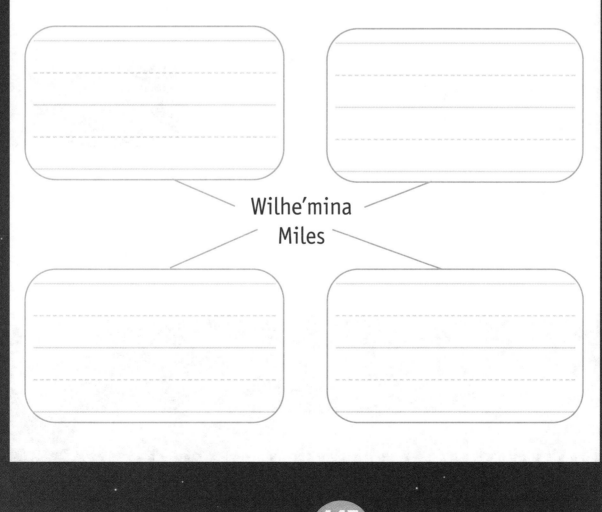

Wilhe'mina
Miles

BEFORE YOU READ

Preview

Before you read, preview the story on page 150 to see what it will be about. Use this checklist to help.

Put an X after you check each one.

PREVIEW CHECKLIST

☐ **Title**

What did you learn from the title?

_____

- -

_____

_____

_____

☐ **Pictures or Photos**

What did you learn from the pictures?

_____

- -

_____

_____

_____

MY PURPOSE

Who is Wilhe'mina Miles and what is she like?

▮▮

STUDYING WORDS: ADDING *ED* AND *ING*

You can add the suffixes *ed* and *ing* to some words.

wait + ed   =   wait**ed**
wait + ing =   wait**ing**
fuss + ing =   fuss**ing**

When words end in a silent *e*, you need to drop the final silent *e* before you add the suffixes *ed* or *ing*.

scare + ed   =   scar**ed**
scare + ing =   scar**ing**

Add *ed* or *ing* to these words. Remember when words end in *e* to drop the final *e* before adding *ed* or *ing*.

1. come + ing =

2. hold + ing =

3. shake + ing =

4. promise + ed =

5. cross + ing =

Now read *Wilhe'mina Miles After the Stork Night* by Dorothy Carter.

1. Read the story all the way through one time.
2. Then come back and read it again. This time, in "My Notes," write a question you have as you read.
3. Then complete the "Stop and Explain" boxes.

My Notes

Example:

Why is she called Sugar Plum?

Wilhe'mina Miles After the Stork Night

by Dorothy Carter

I'm Wilhe'mina Miles, going on eight years old.

Mama says I'm brave and smart.

I used to be called Sugar Plum.

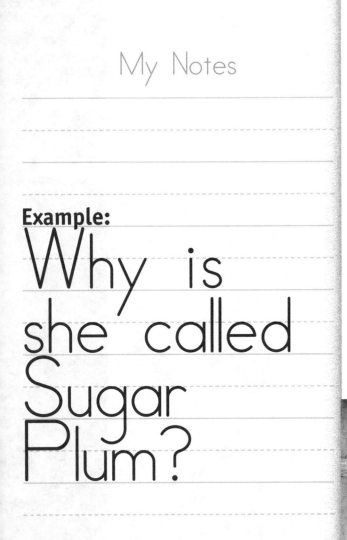

That was my nickname, till one day Mama came home crying. She was holding a letter from my daddy.

"What's the matter, Mama? What's the matter?" I asked.

"Let me pull myself together," she said.

She was heaving and panting hard.

"Your daddy is not coming home as he promised."

Mama threw the letter on the table.

I read, "Sorry, honey bunch, I can't be with you when the stork comes. Soon we'll be together again."

That's all I read.

STOP and EXPLAIN

What did the letter say?

_____

_____

_____

_____

_____

_____

_____

My Notes

_____

_____

_____

_____

_____

_____

_____

_____

_____

_____

WILHE'MINA MILES . . . (continued)

Daddy worked up north at Grand Central Station in New York City.

He sent us money to buy things. This time, Mama bought sheets, new shoes for me, orange gum slices, a sack of chicken feed, and a pink kimono.

Daddy said he was coming home for us soon as he was able.

WILHE'MINA MILES ... (continued)

Mama was always saying how she missed his old brogan shoes airing out on our back porch.

I was tired of waiting, too.

I wanted us to live together the way we used to, before he went to work up north.

He took me fishing at the Trout Creek.

He said, "Sugar Plum, when your cork rises, and you feel a tug and a quiver on your line, you've got a catch. Raise your pole—easy."

That's how it was.

A fish was on the hook.

I didn't want to touch it, flipping and flopping, trying to get back into the water.

My daddy took it off and baited the hook again with a red wiggly worm.

It wasn't long before I could fish just like my daddy.

Soon after Daddy's letter made Mama cry, I had to get Mis' Hattie. Mama begged me to go.

"Please, Sugar Plum, go to Mis' Hattie. Tell her to come at once!"

"The sun's gone down, Mama," I said.

"You stay there with Janey. She'll braid your hair pretty. Be a brave girl and hurry!"

"I'm scared of the dark, Mama."

"The road is bright, girl. Hurry."

"The toad frogs will bite me," I said.

My Notes

"Toad frogs can't bite, Sugar Plum! They just croak and hop. Please hurry! Remember, watch your step on the crossing-over bridge. You'll see the lamplight in Mis' Hattie's window. Go now—run!"

STOP and EXPLAIN

Write what you think will happen next.

These words all have short vowel sounds.

    hat   hen   wish   lock   duck

These words all have long vowel sounds.

    bake   meat   like   boat

Say each of the words below. Decide whether it has a long or short vowel sound. Then write it in the correct box.

bite	**cry**	**run**	**home**
fish	**got**	**catch**	**brave**

Short Vowel Sounds

Long Vowel Sou

Dividing Words with Two Consonants

Many words have two consonants in the middle of them. Often you can divide these words between the consonants.

win / dow   let / ter   pic / ture

Some words have more than two consonants in the middle. Try dividing after the first consonant. If that doesn't help you say the word, try dividing after the second consonant.

Divide the words below into syllables. Draw a line between the two consonants in the middle.

basket   soccer

tadpole   Daddy

matter   Sunday

summer   lesson

III. WRITE

What would you tell Wilhe'mina about you and your family? Write her a letter.

Acknowledgments

8 From *I Am an Apple* by Jean Marzollo. Text copyright © 1997 by Jean Marzollo. Illustrations copyright © 1997 by Judith Moffatt. Reprinted by permission of Scholastic Inc.

18 *Mice Squeak, We Speak* by Tomie dePaola, A Poem by Arnold L. Shapiro. Copyright © 1997 by Tomie dePaola, illustrations. Text copyright © 1984 by World Book, Inc. Original title "I Speak, I Say, I Talk." Used by permission of G.P. Putnam's Sons, A division of Penguin Young Readers Group, A Member of Penguin Group (USA) Inc., 345 Hudson St., New York, NY 10014. All rights reserved.

28 From *Bread, Bread, Bread* by Ann Morris. Text copyright © 1993 by Ann Morris. Photographs copyright © 1993 by Ken Heyman. Used by permission of HarperCollins Publishers.

38 "Sam's Story," from *Three By the Sea* by Edward Marshall, pictures by James Marshall, copyright © 1981 by Edward Marshall, text; copyright © 1981 by James Marshall, pictures. Used by permission of Dial Books for Young Readers, a division of Penguin Young Readers Group, A Member of Penguin Group (USA) Inc., 345 Hudson St., New York, NY 10014. All rights reserved.

52 From *Shoes, Shoes, Shoes* by Ann Morris. Copyright © 1995 by Ann Morris. Used by permission of HarperCollins Publishers.

62 *Building a House* by Byron Barton. Copyright © 1981 by Byron Barton. Used by permission of HarperCollins Publishers.

74 From *Water* by Frank Asch. Copyright © 1995 by Frank Asch, reprinted by permission of Harcourt Inc.

84 From *Too Many Rabbits* by Peggy Parish. © Peppermint Partners.

96 From *Ronald Morgan Goes to Bat* by Patricia Reilly Giff, copyright © 1988 by Patricia Reilly Giff. Used by permission of Viking Penguin, A division of Penguin Young Readers Group, A Member of Penguin Group (USA) Inc., 345 Hudson St., New York, NY 10014. All rights reserved.

106 From *The Golly Sisters Go West* by Betsy Byars. Copyright © 1985 by Betsy Byars. Illustrations copyright © 1985 by Susan G. Truesdell. Used by permission of HarperCollins Publishers.

118 From *Stars: An All Aboard Reading Book* by Jennifer Dussling, illustrated by Mavis Smith, copyright © 1996 by Jennifer Dussling, text. Used by permission of Grosset & Dunlap, A division of Penguin Young Readers Group, A Member of Penguin Group (USA) Inc., 345 Hudson St., New York, NY 10014. All rights reserved.

128 From *Duckling Days* by Karen Wallace (Dorling Kindersley, 1999). Text copyright © Karen Wallace, 1999. Copyright © Dorling Kindersley, 1999.

138 From *Clean Your Room, Harvey Moon!* by Pat Cummings. Reprinted with the permission of Simon & Schuster Books for Young Readers, an imprint of Simon & Schuster Children's Publishing Division from *Clean Your Room, Harvey Moon!* by Pat Cummings. Copyright 1991 Pat Cummings.

150 From *Wilhe'mina Miles After the Stork Night* by Dorothy Carter, pictures by Harvey Stevenson. Text copyright © 1999 by Dorothy Carter. Pictures copyright © 1999 by Harvey Stevenson. Reprinted by permission of Farrar, Straus and Giroux, LLC.

The editors have made every effort to trace the ownership of all copyrighted selections found in this book and to make full acknowledgment for their use. Omissions brought to our attention will be corrected in a subsequent edition.

Book Design: Christine Ronan and Sean O'Neill, Ronan Design

Photographs: Cover © Eileen Ryan Photography, 2003; p. 52 © Ken Heyman–Woodfin Camp & Associates; p. 53 (bottom) © Joe Viesti/Viesti Associates; p. 54 © Ken Heyman–Woodfin Camp & Associates; p. 57 (bottom) © Ariel Skelley/Corbis.

Illustration:
Pages 17, 22: Nicole Wong
Chapter 8: Judy Stead
Chapter 9, pages 5, 32, 35, 56, 72–73, 105, 137: Victor Kennedy
Chapter 11: Burgandy Beam
Chapter 12: Janet Skiles

Developed by Nieman Inc.